Joseph Auslander

RIDERS AT THE GATE

THE MACMILLAN COMPANY
NEW YORK · BOSTON · CHICAGO · DALLAS
ATLANTA · SAN FRANCISCO

MACMILLAN AND CO., Limited
LONDON · BOMBAY · CALCUTTA · MADRAS
MELBOURNE

THE MACMILLAN COMPANY
OF CANADA, Limited
TORONTO

RIDERS AT THE GATE

A Volume of Verse

By Joseph Auslander

1938

THE MACMILLAN COMPANY

New York

PRINTED IN THE UNITED STATES OF AMERICA
AMERICAN BOOK—STRATFORD PRESS, INC., NEW YORK

FOR A. W.

We two have carried the great harp together
That soon enough will break a giant's back;
And though Lord Shakespeare sang in glorious feather,
His shoulder and his voice would sometimes crack;
Heavy upon the single strength between us
We bore the great harp as men bear the Host—
A palanquin for Valentine and Venus,
A cage for Satan and the Holy Ghost.

When, at the difficult hill, my courage faltered,
Your own increased and quickened and replied;
The straight pursuit and struggle never altered
In your proud faith, in your unflagging stride:
Take this faint record of our quest, O sharer
In all, harp-shoulderer and color-bearer!

CONTENTS

CONTENTS

viii

RIDERS AT THE GATE

A ravaged man who leaned upon a staff
And held his heart within his other hand,
And bore upon him dust from every land,
And had a hollow and a mocking laugh,
And at his side a flask whence he did quaff
Drink that was bitter as a faithless friend,
And who was strong, and yet could scarcely stand,
But shook with weakness like a new-born calf;
This man walked up one hill, and down another,
And to himself he muttered many names:
Love, Lust, Hate, War, Mankind and Woman's Brother;
He spoke of Sorrow, and of Wrath that tames
The eagle; but we know not who he was:
See how his footprints burned into the grass!

Write the things which thou hast seen, and the things which
are, and the things which shall be hereafter. . . .
The Revelation of Saint John the Divine
Chapter 1:19

Three riders pull up at the gate;
The flanks of their horses run red;
Each wears a crown on his head:
They are Death and Destruction and Hate.

They do not stop to dismount;
They are gloved in red to the wrist;
They strike on the gate with their fist;
They call the kings to account;

They summon the lords and the keepers
From factory, field and steeple;
From the palaces filled with people
They waken the terrified sleepers;

And the plow is left in the furrow,
And the kettle boils on the fire,
And the servant deserts his hire,
And the archer lets fall his arrow;

And the child, still heavy with dreaming,
Hugs the toy to his bosom;
And the bride whose mouth is a blossom
Starts up from the bridegroom screaming;

And they break the city asunder,
And they put a curse on the towers
That crumple like atrophied flowers,
And the walls of the world go under;

And they shout, as on Patmos the Prophet
Thundered his feverish vision;
And their voice is the scarlet decision
That spatters the altars of Tophet:

This earth to which you cling
By so unsure and fine
A shadow, or a line
Of shadow like a string;

This ball on which you build
Of brick and steel and stone
The little Babylon
Whereby your fears were stilled;

This insubstantial mass
Of water, cloud and dream
Is but a blowing gleam
Of night wind over grass:

For you have long betrayed
Its uses to your lust;
And now you cannot trust
Even the gods you made.

*We are the ancient Four
And the modern merciless Three;
Our mark is on every tree,
And our sign is on every door.*

*You have taken the sword and the spear;
You have split the world with your schisms;
You are filled with the folly of isms;
You have sent for us: we are here.*

*You espouse the spear and the drum;
You forget the horror you made,
Though the blood is wet on the blade.
You call us and we are come.*

*What have you learned since the cave?
And how have you bettered the beast?
You nourish the soil and the priest;
Your bones fatten both in your grave.*

*The wings on your shoulders and ships
You spatter alike with your blood,
And trample the truth in the mud,
And go down with a lie on your lips.*

*Your leaders have entrails of brass;
You feed them your daughters and sons:
They glut the black muzzles of guns;
They clutch red fistfuls of grass.*

Behold the condors that wheel
High over the horsemen of dread;
We stamp on the face of the dead;
They tear it with talons of steel.

You shout, He lives! He is risen!
Our Christian souls He will save!
Then dig Him a fresh grave,
Then build Him a new prison.

You spurn Man's love of the good;
You rant about blood and the race;
You spit on your Savior's face;
You spoil Him and spill His blood.

You mock Man's love of the true,
Man's passion for justice and right;
You hurry him off in the night;
You break his body in two.

You are still what that ancient scribe
Who followed the Eagles of Rome
Distrusted as treacherous scum,
Loathed as a barbarous tribe.

You have not altered one whit:
You are still the fiends of the fen,
Not to be numbered with men,
But devils—and proud of it.

If there were only two,
If there were even one
Straight-standing in the sun,
If there were one of you—

In all the world is none.
We ride from gate to gate;
We find greed, fear and hate;
Of clean hearts never one.

This liberty you boast,
This dream you have denied,
Forever, as we ride,
We glimpse its baleful ghost.

We see it in the Jew
Shot, hounded, raped, reviled;
The little Chinese child
A bayonet ran through.

We see it in the shame
Of nations without pity,
And in the fallen city,
The pillage and the flame.

We see it in the clod,
That once looked like a man,
Mopped up because he ran,
Mowed down because he stood.

RIDERS AT THE GATE

We see the prison camps
Insane messiahs built;
We see the blood they spilt,
The terror as it tramps.

Green shirt, black shirt, brown,
Streaked with the same foul stain,
The bombs that murder Spain,
That cut Abyssinia down.

We see it in the grins
Of madmen in the Alps,
Belted with woolly scalps,
Trophied with ghoulish skins.

We see it in their eyes,
Cruel, crafty and insane,
Gloating on butchered Spain,
Exchanging sugared lies.

(And one will surely start
From sleep, to read his fate,
The Vandal at the Gate,
The Hun's knife at his heart.)

So the Dark Years return,
The Beast is loose in the land:
What you cannot kill, you command;
What you cannot devour, you burn.

Nay, but that nation and nation
Foully consort with the Beast,
And garland his horns, and feast
On the flesh of his fornication!

And eat of the madness of Gath,
Whilst the hungry howl at the gates,
And the young men drop in the streets,
And you guzzle the grapes of His wrath!

Now God grows sick of your follies,
And your wives and daughters a-whoring,
And the stink of their drunken snoring,
And their panders and pimps in your alleys.

You long for the Sabbath to fly.
God's day cannot end too soon,
So you may barter the moon,
And your balances falsify.

So you may grind the poor,
And the face of the beggar refuse,
And sell the cripple for shoes,
And the sick man drive from your door.

You sell your fathers and mothers;
Your sisters will fetch a shilling
To furnish your mouths with swilling,
To heat the minds of your brothers.

You pollute and plunder the Temple,
Bludgeon the priest at his altar,
Dribble his blood on the psalter,
And stain the cloth and the wimple.

And some clotted white hairs adhere
To the ikon that clubbed the Christ:
And the shirtless in Moscow diced,
And Madrid sacked the Sepulchre.

You burn the knowledge you dread;
Men's brains as well as their books;
You turn upon spits and hooks
The truths that will strike you dead.

Your burnings blacken the sky:
The books leave acres of ashes;
But out of the debris flashes
Something no flame can defy.

You herd Life into the breadline;
What love brings forth, you destroy;
You dance in a frenzy of joy
When Death slips under the deadline.

Click, cameras! Spotlights, glare!
Gape, gawk, squeak, jabber, forsooth,
Because the desperate truth
Stands poised on a treacherous stair,

And gulps your coffee and bread
In a quick contemptuous swallow,
And finds your hysterics hollow,
And thumps your cigarette dead,

And, scornful of all the grave meant,
From blood and agony born,
With cold unquenchable scorn
Escapes in a pool on the pavement.

You are frightened and mad, by Mahomet!
You empty your bellies of words;
You snuff them as dogs do their turds;
Like dogs you return to your vomit.

You brag, We are strong, we are able
To straddle the moon in our stride.
And men blurted thus in their pride,
And where is the bombast of Babel?

Though you dig deeper than hell,
And outclimb the morning star,
Our feet will not find it too far,
And there will be nothing to tell.

You split the Tables in half,
Whose Law breathes lightning and thunder;
You bruise, you break and you blunder;
You worship the Golden Calf.

You build the bridge and the boat;
Your vaults bulge silver and gold;
Your justice is bought and sold;
Your synagogue pastures the goat.

Your cunning that rides the air
On horses no wind can master
Shall feed the smoke of disaster,
And the flies your fatness declare;

And the livestock squeal in their stalls,
And the hound howl over his bitch,
And their blood brim a dreadful ditch,
And the nettle possess your halls;

The bittern and cormorant come,
The owl and the raven sit
On the rafters and ruin of it,
And the lion call it his home;

And the thorn be king in your courts,
And queen of your desolation,
And the wild pig's habitation,
And the screech owl scream from your forts.

Behold the Juggernaut Wagon:
Smith, bandit, and paperhanger
Grind you to dust in their anger,
Sowing the teeth of the Dragon.

Cringest thou from the lash
Of the little lunatic Thor
Who spouts and sputters of war
Under his comic moustache?

Fearest thou Caesar's threat,
The thrust of that thick blue jowl,
The glare, the grimace and the growl,
The bomb and the bayonet?

Tremblest thou under the weight
Of Ivan the Terrible's smile,
Dreading the torturer's guile,
His love far more than his hate?

Have you not seen these before,
In Athens, Jerusalem, Rome?
In Babylon's golden dome
Heard not Behemoth roar?

Gog and Magog again,
And Moloch's infernal brood,
The Beast and his brotherhood
Hatched in Beelzebub's brain?

Comfort you, then; be assured
Their flesh will fatten the soil,
Their bones run marrow like oil,
The fields with their filth be manured.

These who have cheapened life,
Debased the spirit of man,
Ennobled the charlatan,
Taken the Terror to wife;

Rendered to Caesar the things
That pertain to God, and anew
Made a whipping boy of the Jew,
And fed the kites with your kings;

These who erect their hate
Into a monstrous art,
Pander the personal heart
In whoredom to the State;

And fortify their fear
By twisting the young from truth,
Leaving the whole world's youth
Impaled upon the spear:

These shall not long delay
In the sun, these barbarous lords
Running amok with their swords—
The wind shall blow them away.

The firing squad shall not miss them;
The top-hatted headsman not fail them;
The hound and the hoot-owl shall hail them;
And the axe's tongue tickle and kiss them.

Though not before nations are bled
Stark white of their blood and treasure,
Milked and drained without measure
In the holocaust of the dead.

For once more the cannon shall cough,
And bodies explode like rockets,
And eyeballs burst from their sockets,
And heads go mushrooming off;

And the shocked air rock and rattle,
Horizons shake like huge pulses,
While the red earth convulses,
And captains and horses and cattle

Churn in a weltering ooze
And choke the nostrils with stink,
And the streams from which you drink
Heave boots and scummed green shoes;

And bandages stiffen with blood,
And the surgeon's baskets slop over,
And shapeless things writhe to cover,—
And the Three Horsemen thud.

For once more the Riders ride,
And the poisonous aftermath scorches,
And the drenched cairns blaze like torches,
And the world splits from side to side;

And the steel wasps drone and deliver,
And horses, gun carriages, men
Are blown into pieces again,
And the great holes vomit forever;

And the torn trees leap, and the horses
Trample their entrails; the ground
Spins the red whirlpool around
In an orgy of nightmarish forces.

From the clumps of flesh jut fingers
And tufts of hair; grim cones
Of hurriedly carbonized bones—
And the reek unnameable lingers.

And the night, the corrosive rain,
The puddle of muck and metal,
The corpses that rise, and settle,
And rise, and settle again.

Abhorred of the greatest and least,
And flushed with a horrible fever,
The Horsemen who gallop forever
Go raging before the Beast.

And a seal of the Book is broken,
And that horse is heralded first,
Of whom the horseman is curst,
Whose hoof scatters Hate for a token.

And the second seal bursts, loosing forth
The horse and the horseman whose mouth
Drops blood and flame east and south,
Bellows War in the west and the north.

And the third seal splits, and a breath
Announces the pale horse and one
Who grins through a lattice of bone,
And the horse and the rider are Death.

The first mad horseman Hate
Slobbers through gleeful lips;
And the froth drools and drips
Green and degenerate.

Close after him that pair
Of brutish and fetid savor—
The Battle and the Cadaver,
Whose horror hangs in the air.

And a Fourth Horseman rides,
And throws on the gruesome three
A shadow bigger than he,
And behind that shadow he hides.

And the name of that rider is Hope,
And he is God's seventh son,
The last, and the merciful one,
Whose mercy no man may escape.

Even the Scarlet Whore
Of the world, the Babylon Strumpet
Found hope in his hushed trumpet,
Though the riders dinned on the door.

He, when his brothers stood,
Flame-tressed, and trumpeted
Earth and sea blood-red,
And the sky red as blood,

And all that therein are,
All things that are therein;
He, only, left the din
And watched the falling star;

Saw our sweet world go down,
Man's beauty and his pride
Brushed like a moth aside,
And his mind overthrown.

Fiercely his eyes he kept
Fixed on man's Pentecost,
And thought, All is not lost,
And hid his eyes, and wept

As One, years later, keeping
Such vigil in such place
Suddenly covered His face
And fled Jerusalem weeping.

Beautiful are the veins that twist
And meet like stitches of blue thread
To set a flower in your wrist
Softly distributed.

Who are you that can thus relate
A legend lovelier than the rose?
That in your blood so delicate,
So blue a flower blows?

Are you the Princess in the tale
Whom brigands kidnapped at her birth,
Whose hands like holy lamps prevail
Against our graceless earth?

Are you the girl whose lover died
Last night to hold a hill for Spain?
Are you this morning's suicide
Pulled dripping from the Seine?

Are you the child in the factory
Whose fingers dart like knitted light?
Are you the girl I always see
Laughing in parks at night?

Are you, like freedom, man's bright hunger?
Are you, like hope, a bitter bread?
The song we sing to stand up stronger?
The words that wake the dead?

Ah, surely once amid the faggots
I saw you glow against the flame;
And when the Man rose from the maggots
I heard Him call your name.

Ah, surely in prophetic sand
It was your fiery finger wrote;
And yesterday it was your hand
That gripped the tyrant's throat.

And that blue-latticed wrist, that hand
Will man's beleaguered birthright save;
Tomorrow with the truth will stand
Between him and the grave.

Slugs stir abroad; the air is alive with dew;
The young cock's crooked tenor cracks at C;
And at this moment, somewhere in Germany,
A man is shot because he is a Jew.

Domestic bickers flutter hen and pullet;
The pearly channel of the worm shows plain;
And at this moment, in a ditch in Spain,
A black hole in the heart applauds a bullet.

Terror scratches a match on ragged teeth
And screams with laughter in a limpid sky
To see the Chinese children sprawled awry,
To read the ghastly caption underneath.

I turn, half-blinded from the battle,
To other and far happier cattle,
Whose fly-nicked fetlocks plash the water
We will pollute some day with slaughter.
All day, each day, the cattle pass
From field to field, from grass to grass;
At noon they stand beneath the trees
Like figures in a Grecian frieze;
Before the night is half-way over
They feast on quietness and clover;
They slumber, but they never make
Promises the dawn will break;
Whilst we, who from our terrors creep
Into an ambush men call sleep,
Will suddenly with a great groan start,
Impaled upon the hopeless heart.

And but for whom this world were dull indeed,
A swamp where maggots swarm and mayflies blow,
Save that the world knew April long ago,
Save that you plucked a common wayside weed,
Mullein or rag, and shaped it to a reed,
And put your breath to it and made it know
Hamlet and daffodil and Romeo,
Ophelia and the heartbreak laugh of Lear,
And the Fool's prattle driving a dark spear
Into our throats . . . and from your English glades
The bird that storms the morning's barricades
Forever. . . . Ah, were you here now to sing
April's white face and tragic eyes this spring!

We are driven, but we cannot vanish;
We are trampled, but we will not yield:
Chinese, Ethiopian, Spanish,
The Jew on his shield.

By fire and sword we are scattered;
By murder they seek to affright us:
We survive the Wall that is shattered,
The terror of Titus.

Our dreams can endure their derision,
Our hopes make light of their laughter,
Strong in the strength of the Vision
Here and hereafter.

Whom Sheba and Solomon cherish;
Whose Law builds a fortress about them;
No kin of Confucius shall perish,
No horrors can rout them.

Once more Don Quixote is riding,
And bright is the banner he flashes,
And the fierce heart of Spain is abiding
The blood and the ashes.

Beleaguered, we will not surrender;
Bombs, burnings, blockades cannot break us:
Faith will raise up the defender
Who will not forsake us:

Faith in the issue of battle
Which consecrates man and his neighbor
To fight the blind furies that rattle
The chains and the saber;

Faith against hatred that hisses
At man, that confounds to confusion
The love of mankind and dismisses
Such love as delusion.

Not the local crusade of one nation
This trumpet to battle, nor solely
For self, but for man's preservation,
For humankind wholly.

And this faith must hearten and guide us,
This challenge we take and we cherish:
For how and what stronghold shall hide us
If liberty perish!

These are the wounds that bleed forever:
The trampling of a dream in dust;
The fettering of free endeavor
By fear and hate, by pride and lust.

These are the wounds too deep for dying:
The strangling of the storms of youth;
The fist that strikes an infant crying;
The laughter frozen on the mouth.

These are the wounds that will not alter,
Though frightened tongue and hand submit:
The spirit broken to the halter;
The freedom roped into the pit.

These are the wounds too strong for stopping,
These are the wounds that must not heal:
The heart's blood of the martyr dropping
Under the tyrant's chariot wheel.

Once I set great store by books,
Men's promises and women's looks,
A fancy tie, a foreign hat
And things like that.

Now I had rather dine at home
On bread and broken honeycomb;
Engage the oak's green company,
Or smell the sea;

Or glimpse the speckled golden guest,
All appetite, in robin's nest,
And know, in spite of Hitler's hell,
The world is well;

And know, when Mussolini lies,
A bloated banquet for the flies,
The wild white heron, screaming harsh,
Will haunt the marsh;

And know that there is peace to find
Far past the mischief of the mind,
Hearing the spring's first peeper cuddle
His rain-pocked puddle:

And, taking heart from these, rejoice
In realms beyond man's fist and voice,
Beyond his works and words, above
His hate, his love.

CONQUEROR WORM

And how shall any satrap long escape?
And what assurance stronger than a mouse
Can our morticians give the hordes that gape
On holy Lenin in his marble house?
And where shall Mussolini, were he bigger
Than his Colossus, hope at length to hide
His huge contempt for some contemptuous nigger
Who spits upon the dust he once defied?

The mountebank messiah, though he mutter
A thousand maledictions in his beer
And drag his people with him to the gutter,
Shall not elude his executioner
The Worm who, if the formal top hat lacks,
Still boasts a tooth more thorough than the axe.

Poet of Chillon! Prince of the oppressed!
We need your trumpet's voice for, still confined,
Man rots in vicious dungeons of the mind,
Fettered to savage passions which infest
Like worms and vipers his immortal breast:
For we are still as brutal and as blind,
And still with sordid treacheries we bind
The burning spirit of the heart's behest.

The wolfish pack that snarled at Bonnivard
And howled you out of England is the same,
Nor have their tactics altered, save in name:
By stealth, by ambush, by the tricks of war
They flourish, stalking friend and foe alike,
Their vile fangs fouling what they dare not strike!

This heap of loose discolored stones
Drank the blood from ancient bones;

Saw the Druid hold his knife
Naked at the heart of life;

Heard the shrill chant break where stood
Caesar's Eagles bright as blood;

And the black-robed women screaming,
And their wild red tresses streaming,

And the painted heathen faces,
And the broken spears and traces,

And the shaggy horses crying,
And the mounds of dead and dying,

And the solid Roman wall—
Heard it all and saw it all:

Even as I hear and see
Darker human agony;

Even as I see and hear,
In the springtime of the year,

Drench of blood and dripping sword
These had never seen or heard.

For the whole world round is one
Steaming sacrificial stone;

One carnage in a crimson wood
For some dubious brotherhood.

Than these dead stones I know far less
Of our commingled nothingness.

Despair deep in the mind
Hooks his venomous dart;
I pluck it, only to start
The stream its kiss confined.

So do these friends contrive—
The slayer and the slain,
The poison and the pain—
To keep each other alive.

A BLACK SONNET

Time is an interval between events
Whereof the end and the beginning seem
Familiar to the maggot, but a dream
To man, devoid of cause and consequence.
From sun to shadow we make measurements;
From birth to death compute a fading beam;
In both our cradles an occasional scream
Commemorates a dark coincidence.

Free of this world and of that other, we
Go shambling miserably ill at ease,
Splendid with medals, ragged at the knees,
At home in neither world, and never free,
Stammering hymns to keep us from confusing
The Heaven we lost, the Hell beyond our losing.

To see this flame of life, this flow
Of mass and color, glance and glow
Of slitted eyes and the masked laughter
Behind the dotted domino;

To know that men can make believe
Though despots growl and captives grieve;
That still in brief impossible gardens
The innocent snake can dance with Eve—

This comforts, though it cannot bless
For long a world grown comfortless;
How can the fiddles quench the fire?
How beat the blaze with a spangled dress?

And yet, perhaps, if the whole world rang
With music, if the mad world sang
Suddenly, Rome might cease from burning,
And the battle-axe no longer clang.

For song has saved the world before,
And Momus routed the God of War,
And the flash of sequins, the flare of laughter
Frightened the wolf from the falling door.

Darkly the treacherous panegyric
The corpse-deep victory announces
By hoarse hurrah, by bellowing lyric,
By medal packed with pompous ounces.

Trophies and monuments attest,
Far from the carnage and the shame,
Far from the hero's shell-plowed breast,
The folly of a posthumous fame.

Unterrified and urgent still,
Willow and warbler both presume,
By leaf and feather, bough and bill,
To question man's archaic doom.

When nations at their Christmas Feast
The Prince of Good Will consecrate,
Whilst the Apocalyptic Beast
Rages in horror and in hate,
How shall they reconcile these two,
If two such can be reconciled:
How seat the Gentile with the Jew?
How feed the Chinese—and the Child?

Oh how, upon the holy plate,
Between the candles of the Lord,
Shall we commingle Love and Hate?
How carve His banquet with the sword?
Or by what self-deception mix
Water with blood to mimic wine?
What lies can cleanse the crucifix
To stop its dripping on the Shrine?

Let no tongue of the Jesu prattle
Or sprinkle sugary condiments;
Not when our very windows rattle
With bombs that slaughter Innocents.
Not in such fashion dare we burnish
A single straw to ease Her head,
Who by Her love alone did furnish
The stable God inhabited.

There is no middle course to follow,
No clever furtive compromise;
The Christmas Carol rings too hollow
In dead men's ears, at dead men's eyes:
Either we stand with Christ in hell,
And His faith brevets our behavior;
Or muffle the drum and drape the bell,
And perish, Christian, with your Savior!

Fears heavier than mountains press
Upon the Sleeper's sleeplessness;
And harder than a stone the bed,
The pillow that supports His head.
The lightest portion of man's hate
Can over-tip a mountain's weight;
And there are stones that will not move
Except for some terrific love.
Every time a whipt dog moans,
We add a stone to all His stones;
Every heart that cries aloud,
Jew and Gentile, crushed and cowed,
Children maimed and mutilated,
People hounded, people hated,
People herded, spat on, driven
By a lash that snarls at heaven—
All of these, and more beside:
Vicious envy, cruel pride,
Venomous little coiled-up lusts,
Cold suspicions, dark distrusts,
Revenges vile, and jealousies
Curdling in the blood they freeze.
Every black and bitter word,
Every slaughtered beast and bird,
Griefs that fester, greeds that smoulder
Pile fresh stones upon Christ's shoulder;
Our own craven cowardice
Equal cuts with Judas' kiss;
Wheresoever men are weak,
One Man turns the other cheek;

Every duty we evade
Is a burden on Him laid;
Over His bent back are draped
Consequences we escaped;
Every city shelled and taken,
Every citadel forsaken,
Every foe and every friend
His to vanquish—and defend.
So, forever torn apart
By the great love in His heart,
Every moment, night and day,
That love wears some stone away;
Forever and forever rolls
Rocks from other burdened souls,
Giving to the least of these
His strength, His sleep and His lost peace.

Never let cautious Time put Truth to tether,
Play out the rope, restrict the reckless colt—
The moon-splash on his forehead, Satan's feather
Blown over eyes that sparkle hot revolt.
Nor cut his violent mouth on Wisdom's bridle,
Nor curb his fury with a thoughtful spur,
Nor clap upon his back the coward's saddle
Whose heart was smithied by Prince Lucifer.

This is no ambling pad, no pretty jennet
With jingling bells and gentle mincing pace
To jiggle some sweet maiden lady's bonnet,
Or joggle one curl loose across her face;
This is the horse of Hell : behold the proof
Printed in blood beneath that dreadful hoof!

The apple that fell on Newton's nose
Might just as well have been a feather
Dropped from that bird whose breast is a burning rose,
Beauty and Truth on a single luminous tether
Falling together.

This fruit by some celestial error
Slipped from the sleepy fist of the sun;
Or the bright Phoenix flaming like a mirror
Upon the shoulder of heaven fluttered one
Feather down.

Not any foreordained event
Nailed big upon God's bulletin board,
But only a neat enormous accident—
An apple, or a feather, that fell toward
That nose—and scored!

Much comfort lingers in the allegory,
That whoso snores beneath a tree may find
His name enrolled among the sons of glory,
An apple, or a theory, on his mind—
Or both combined.

Joist and girder tell the truth,
Singing it from shore to shore;
Not a simile uncouth,
Not a clouded metaphor.

Here glows tyranny of line,
And the Fraction sits with God;
Logic, cruel and divine,
Squares the even with the odd.

Hairbreadth Error breaks its back,
(Buttresses as well were straw);
Annihilation hides the crack
Truth never saw.

I understand too well how that old Greek,
Footsore and famished for his native skies,
Could scarcely breathe nor trust his tongue to speak
When the Aegean burst upon his eyes.
The peacock moon spreads cold upon the sea
As in a mirror his enormous fan;
My heart is glass to such idolatry,
And in his shadow I grow more than man.

So Greek and moon and any man, with tide
At full and churning thickly to the light,
Become a part of one fierce joy so wide
It touches the anatomy of night,
And stops the breath and leaves upon the tongue
The taste of something old when God was young.

ACKNOWLEDGMENT

Were you my mother, sea, I could not come
With quieter assurance to your breast,
Feeling like some old sailor carried home,
After long absence, home to his heart's rest;
Were you my sister, sea, I could not find
A welcome easier to a wanderer's feet,
A benediction to a clouded mind,
The holy bells of heaven ringing sweet.

Were you my friend, I could not love you more;
My enemy, I could not love you less;
All these you are, and these have been before—
Mother and sister, hate and friendliness:
Perhaps I love you best when, like a friend,
You give me honest anger at the end.

As one who in a desert finds the dew;
Or, doomed to exile worse than death among
A barbarous people and a guttural tongue,
Suddenly hears a song his childhood knew
In Athens, and can scarce believe it true;
Or, as a captive into daylight flung
From darkness and the sulphur pits and dung;
Or as a warm bed to the Wandering Jew:

So to the sea's child in the city street,
Moving with hurried hostile folk, apart,
The thunder of the tides comes loud and sweet,
The herring gull, the sea hawk suddenly start
Because a pigeon flutters at his feet,
Because a feather sweeps across his heart.

A shell the Goddess would not scorn
She brought as trophy from the sea:
The pearly couch that might have borne
Venus Anadyomene.

She laid her treasure in my hand,
Jewels wrought by time and water;
Herself the noblest that could stand
Before men, Aphrodite's daughter.

Into my human grasp she laid
The trident locked in Neptune's fist,
The horn on which old Triton played,
The bracelet from a Nereid's wrist.

She gave these glories to my keeping,
Into my custody she gave
The couch that bore her Mother sleeping,
The shell that marked her Mother's grave.

Forsythia blows away;
It is pale glory:
So the most golden day
Is a forgotten story;
For all that we can say
It will not stay.

Once, in your garden blowing,
I watched the golden shower,
As now I see it glowing
In this impatient hour;
As now I mark its going,
A starry snowing.

So fairest flowers decay;
So love is taken
In a brief holiday;
So the faint gold is shaken
From the forsythia spray
Down and away.

These are the reconciliations of the spring:
The bird and the bough,
The tree and the leaf,
The earth and the plough,
Man and his grief—
But never man and himself, alas, ah, never this thing.

These are the perennial truces of time and weather:
The sun and the seed,
The wind and the sail,
The song and the reed,
The hammer and nail—
But never man and his own, never man and his brother.

The city has yawned its people out; forlorn
The streets; the sidewalks blank and flatulent;
A wagon rattles; an occasional horn
Honks; the sun's disk is a battered cent.

This is a sordid little wilderness;
And from their iron nests with a dead flutter
The pigeons drop, falling in a gray S
To peck at theatre programs in the gutter.

What do they know of holiday or heaven,
Or picnics in the country under leaves,
Or the sea churning up a silver leaven,
Or anything but gutters and grim eaves?

They should be far from this mad empty house;
The green grove is their birthright: they should be
Cathedralled in a tower of gothic boughs,
Or prove their wings in boundless liberty.

But we have snared them from their bright domain;
Alien and listless in our world they go,
Tapping at stone like blind men with a cane . . .
But it is Sunday—and they do not know.

Worm-puller, with breast as red
As a suicide's coat,
How fine the tilt of your head,
The taunt of your throat!

What anchored economy
Compels the tight No,
The rooted tenacity
Of earth letting go!

Yet rootless man remains,
And man's brave hope
That tugs at terrible chains,
That tests their scope,

Nor stops for breath, nor stands
One instant still,
The blood upon its hands
For good or ill;

The heart proud and infirm,
And hope that feeds it;
The heart that is hope's worm,
And hope that bleeds it;

Hope straining at the heart
No hope can cherish;
And neither daring to part,
Lest both perish.

I go content
With time misspent,
Watching the days
Distil a phrase:
Recurrent dawn
Add her great noun;
And midday curb
With level verb
That gallant one,
The hot-mouthed sun;
And evening give
Her adjective,
Her quiet moon
To cool the noon;
And sleep, like God,
Write period.

Sleep is a tunnel that dwindles to a dot
Down in the mind;
Sleep is a keyhole we fumble with hands hot,
Eyes blind;
Sleep is a make-believe gate in a make-believe garden
In a valley near falling water we never find.

INTERREGNUM

These are the long and noisy adjournments of August,
The grassy sessions, the lingering parliaments,
Crickets in filibuster, and the locusts
Crowding a fervent congress in the sun;
These are the mortal moments of the wasp
Whose papery lanterns crumple in the gust;
The sparrows at impromptu caucus creaking
On telegraph wires; the drowsy bulletins
Of flies; the two swans arguing on the lake;
Rugs on the porch chairs powdered damp with twilight;
And the snail writing *Finis* in wet silver.

The thunder talked a little while;
Between its phrases we talked on.
Its huge head blotted out the sun;
Yet we could sit, and we could smile,

And lift our careful cups of tea.
The lightning paused to stand and stare,
And whirl its long blue whips of hair,
And choose a steeple or a tree.

Black and baleful in our breasts
(Though doors are built to fasten out
The lightning-scream, the thunder-shout)
They brood like uninvited guests.

And they have entered stealthily
Upon this ominous afternoon;
And china clinking against spoon
Stirs up a turbulent cup of tea.

One afternoon the poet found
That brief retreat where Autumn kneeled,
Burning as on holy ground,
Naked in a stubblefield,
Her forehead with the poppies crowned,
The great sun-dappled breasts revealed.

Autumn with hot coppery hair,
And heavy lids and heavy mouth,
And sunburnt throat and bosom bare
And brown and bright as the breasts of Ruth,
Still kneels in that corn-dusty air
And shades a gold-flecked longing south.

And Keats, to whom the sun confides
Her single truth, her simple trust,
In her pavilion still abides,
His eyes still dazzled with her lust;
And he shall sing her vespertides
Till song and sun alike are dust.

The cold wind combs the marsh's hair
And curdles the combed sea
Livid bluewhite like the underfur
Of birds on a blowing tree.

It asks me not if I be young,
Or beautiful, or wise,
Or if I speak a thrifty tongue,
Or spout enormous lies.

It questions not my need or name,
Whatever name or need;
But licks my wounds with icy flame
And flogs me till I bleed.

Ah, sweeter far this forthright gust
Than man's most honeyed breath
That lashes at the heel of trust
The lightning inch of death.

Here no deception lurks, no smile
Fixed on the face of hate;
No sugared prologue to beguile
The scissors of man's fate.

But only wind and water blown,
Wind and water blowing
For one man out of a world alone,
For one man's going.

Like any man to whom the knife
Seems an exit less than proud,
And the bullet much too loud
A valedictory to life,

I look upon the blasted tree,
The blistered circle on the heath;
The twinkling little mice of death
In the lightning's hair I see.

And I see upon the ground
Broken wing and shattered nest,
And the ruin manifest
Where the lightning ran around;

Where the lightning on all fours
Ran and sniffed, the lightning ran
Like a crooked kind of man,
Like a crazy kind of horse.

And the lightning in the brain
Scampers brightly with despair;
But upon the ruin there
Almost never falls the rain.

Monotonously the anonymous locust writes
His hot insistent signature whose verb
With one metallic midday noun unites
To comfort and disturb.

He shapes the multisyllabled summer's chant
To singular, that else were murmuring mist
Of vowel and promiscuous consonant,—
O princely plagiarist!

No argument invades his universe :
Spaniard and Russian both can understand
The candid ritual his thighs rehearse,
The music of his wand.

This early autumn evening is a bell
Clapperless, yet all compact of sound,
Like the inaudible water in some well
A fathom underground.

No crypt or cloister can such peace maintain:
The cricket in the dripping grass, the leaf
Released, the finely sieved consent of rain,
The spider's handkerchief.

I will break bread with that old man, Li Po,
Get drunk upon his poems and his wine,
Observe the grass with Whitman and Thoreau,
And take their hearts to mine.

I cannot find my tongue with clever men,
Nor write my time nor wrestle with the age;
I turn to autumn and this evening's rain,
And put them on a page.

Our love is like a meadow in the sun,
A little island in the marshy grass,
A limpid mirror for oblivion,
And for the steel-blue heron a smooth glass;
The straight reed, the unrippled osier,
The starry water-hyacinth softly stand;
The six gold goslings paddling here and there
Maintain a guard upon this holy land.

Never the swan, never the nightingale
Disturb this liquid outpost of illusion;
Nor man with his old melancholy tale
Of conscience, restlessness and loud confusion;
But love at peace that pricks the noiseless braille
Of heron on the sand without conclusion.

The river is divided
By sun and cloud in two:
Half where the blaze shot through,
Half where the black abided.

Between two lights we stand;
We move from grace to grace,
The wings upon your face,
Their shadow on my hand.

I will mount with the moon her tremendous tidal horses,
Turbulent stallions foaled from the same fierce mother,
Rushing forever toward and away from each other,
Forever plunging along the moon-clocked courses.

My fate in love I will bind to the moon's great wheel,
Content with the tidal yoke to undergo
The fall of passion after passion's flow,
And what I cannot understand, to feel.

Arise, my love, my fair one, and come away:
For the combers gleam with phosphor-bearded light,
And the tide runs high at half-past nine tonight,
And tomorrow is another night and day.

We will find all manner of curious fluted shells
With intricate patterns to keep Cellini awake;
We will leave a few on the beach for the boys to take;
We will reek of kelp, sea kale and brackish smells.

Rise up, my love, for the sandpipers are running
Three to each gull along the water's edge;
Twilight's at hand: we've had the sun's hot pledge
From early dawn; we've had our fill of sunning.

Arise, my love, the sun sleeps in your pocket;
I'll slip a string of stars around your wrist:
Now shut your eyes and think of amethyst,
And at your throat the moon will hang her locket.

AFTERMATH

From passionate reproach and wolfish quarrel,
When great convulsions rage and rains drive dark
And gouts of blood bespatter bay and laurel,
No dove of peace will perch upon the ark;
But churned up from our anger, blind and heated,
Upon the heart hurled far along the sand
Strange deep-sea growths, primordial and fetid,
Will fasten to enrich the heart's demand.

Torn from her wharf, the heart through hours of horror
Finds heavy peace high on some foreign shore:
So, as the glorious morning star glows clearer,
The wracked deep washes to our very door
No seagreen mermaid sunning in her mirror,
But slow sea-spittle and the tawny spore.

No less than this loud sea, Love has her tides,
And no less loud and none the less confined
Beneath the moon in man's uneasy mind
Which without heat compels, with light decides
Coldly the rhythm each quick impulse rides;
Nor heart nor brain is kind, as men know kind:
Reason is heartless and the heart is blind,
And one forever chafes, one ever chides.

O constant turmoil! O inconstant heart!
Storm in the blood and tempest in the brain,
And in the mind perpetual hurricane
That tears the fabric of the soul apart:
Yet from such tides spawn scholars and skyscrapers,
Music and murder and this morning's papers.

Heap as on a prince's plate
Hissing still the feast of hate
Though it prove a surly meat,
I am not afraid to eat;
Love grown stale and soft and sure
Rises from this feast secure,
Stronger for such honest fare,
Newly fortified to bear
Once again the dish that by it
Seems less treacherous a diet.

Because my love lies underneath
The bough whose heavy bloom is shed,
I will keep the birds from death,
I will give them crusts of bread.

Let them hop upon her hand,
Let them walk upon her face;
Every bird in this bleak land
Come and eat the bread of grace.

Though the wind howls in the nest,
Though the earth is hard and black,
Here is bread, and it is blest,
Here is love, and let none lack.

Strange that gold which crumbles not,
Makes the heart that hugs it rot;
Incorruptible, its kiss
Corrupts the lord whose slave it is,
Till the worm within the grave
Eats whom gold could never save,
And from eyelids webbed with sleep
Drop the coins he could not keep.

Only love that hoards each kiss
With a kingly avarice
Leaves, when mouths are black with mould,
Hearts whose metal shames the gold;
Love, whose misers grip intact
In a single heart's beat packed,
Safe from rain, secure from rust,
Ransom glowing in the dust.

Who pledges the pure metal of Love's truth
Gives coinage glowing with the god's own face,
Not to be dulled by Time's promiscuous tooth,
But lighted with the lord's immediate grace.
And whoso carries, pressed into his palm,
This image of the god, stamped bright in gold,
In spite of tumults, keeps a shining calm,
In spite of grey hairs, he will not grow old.
Such love could bribe the stubborn gates of hell,
Flatter the callous and accustomed fist
Of the grim ferryman, his hound as well,
And coax the raven from Night's rigid wrist;
And wring from Death himself a prompt reprieve,
Being too beautiful a thing to leave.

PENTECOST

Only a few upon their shoulders feel
The feathered implications time has crushed,
The sense of tumults tugging at the heel,
Of wings and victories forever hushed.
This is the secret buried in our birth,
As old as tides of memory, and as new;
Yet seldom in the dusty round of earth
Do hints of that lost heritage come true.

And then across the marshes of despair,
Into our dreamless misery intrudes
A grace as strong as starlight in the air,
A music pure as the Beatitudes:
And in the streets the people stop and stare,
Guessing the glory that above them broods.

Ho, then, here,
Chanticleer!
You and I
In the night
Read the sky,
Black or bright,
Watch it thicken,
Shift and quicken:
And your beak
And my lip
In a bleak
Partnership
Now unite,
Now announce,
Now pounce
On the light.

For our kin
Find no rest;
Hand to chin,
Beak at breast,
They malinger
And they mock,
Till the singer,
Till the cock
Join their throats,
Blend their bugles,
Blow their notes
Brave as eagles.

And they know,
Man and fowl,
Light will flow,
Feed the soul.
Frightened feather,
Frantic hand
Both together
Understand.

This ceiling, where wheels roll and pass
In shadows of refracted light,
As in a highly polished glass:
Impromptu page, where day and night
Their unenduring pageant write;

This mirror, even as I look,
Where night and day their names record;
Where traffic scrolls a silent book;
Where, tender, tragic and absurd,
The morning climbs without a word—

I think it not unlikely so
The flashes of the prophets come:
Nothing to see and less to show,
And yet a brief Byzantium
Is now and then vouchsafed to some.

Give the Waterbusters back
What turned their fathers' blue skies black,
Bruised the cloud and made it crack.
Give them their Thunderbird again,
Their Sacred Bundle big with rain.
Soon or late Science must
Bow before the blinding dust,
Fold its desks and close its doors,
Yield to Faith the desert floors,
Superstition's ancient chores
Of letting loose the heavy rain,
Of hanging tassels on the grain,
Of bringing bread out of pain.
When human cheeks and hopes grow hollow,
When drouth bleaches corn and cattle,
Let the Waterbusters bellow,
Let the Sacred Bundle rattle.
While professors ponder charts
Let the rain revive men's hearts.

SALVE ATQUE VALE

Ah surely this is not the end,
And in our hearts he is not dead;
He was our neighbor and our friend
Whose wisdom danced in what he said,
Whose understanding comforted.

Old Plato found him in his youth
And nourished his immortal mind,
Like a green cedar set in truth,
For shade and for delight designed,
Expansive, tolerant and kind.

His place is empty in our hall,
And at our table he is gone;
He will not answer when we call,
And with our questions he is done;
Our laughter dies against a stone.

Hail and Farewell and Hail once more,
Friend of the twinkling eyes and brain.
We glimpse your shadow through the door
Your shadow shall not pass again;
We hear the wind, we hear the rain.

This boy, this girl, whose feet in marble stand,
Their fingers fastened to a cloud of stone,
Each embracing each with heavy hand
Less free than blood, more permanent than bone:
Like dancers in some ponderous pantomime,
Shod with intolerable grace they move
Within a moveless area of time,
Locked in the long reluctance of their love.

Only the dense inertia of their fate
Compels this passion, mouth to cold mouth pressed,
The stubborn throat, the kiss that bears no weight,
The soundless heart, the stony-feathered breast.
Here youth shall never shed the plumes of pride,
Nor bridegroom turn him to a younger bride.

Under the withering funeral wreath
Pismire and pigweed riot;
Still in the glassy stare of death
Smoulders what nothing can quiet.

Still the redundant rose is flung
On yesterday's flinger of roses;
Out of the songs the singer had sung
Another, and better, composes.

In the dawn's murk the armies tramp
That by noon will be dead or dying;
But their boots may startle up from the swamp
A moon-white heron crying.

Some men must die like Lazarus, all sores,
Blind, in great agony, with blistered lips,
Their bandaged fists dull red from beating doors
In vain—until the ground beneath them slips;
And others lash their souls with savage whips
Of questions without answers, till the floors
Of reason fall like oceans with wrecked ships
That heave forever between phantom shores.

And others still must climb upon the dead,
Or step upon the dying, till they reach
The peephole where a thousand others bled
To stare across a wild and dreadful beach
Black with the squadroned buzzards overhead,
Shaking their wings and shrieking, each to each.

II.

We are like Lazar, rocking on the brink
Of this harsh world that bears men in its womb;
No less than mayflies we as well must blink
In the cold light that streaks a broken tomb.
Only in earth we find sufficient room,
Content our eyes with darkness thick as ink,
Into our mouths accept medicinal doom,
And with our minds the deaths of kingdoms drink.

Yet always the fierce formula of spring
Cancels our silence and invades our sleep,
Till man once more becomes a restless thing,
And on bruised hands and knees begins to creep
Out of his grave, the blood still on his wing,
And in blind eyes the pledge he could not keep.

Where is the god of the thick green thumb
Who makes the grass and the green corn come?
Who spreads on the parched and tortured land
Like a great green hope a great green hand?
Who packs hot gold into Kansas wheat?
The hot gold honey of Kansas heat;
Who fingers the earth till the earth springs green
With flowers and fruits and birds between;
Whose green thumbnail can scratch dead ground
Till it shoots green showers for miles around?
Every stick or stone that green thumb strikes
Spurts suddenly splendid with bright green spikes.
God of the green touch, press your thumb
On our burnt-out hearts till the green thoughts come;
Till the black shell splits, and the green flame starts,
Keep your thumb on our thoughts, keep your hand on our
    hearts.

OASIS

This grassy innocence, and the sun,
And the heifer's side like watered silk,
And the way the smut-faced lambkins run
And totter, tugging the teats for milk,
And the way the world is never done;

And the globs of gold in the pan of cream,
And the bubbly gold in the churning vat,
And the livestock stalls and the dewy steam
That beads the fresh-curled butter pat,
And the frost-nippled pitcher fresh from the stream—

Whatever mercy the heart may procure
From the treacherous mind that infests the brain,
Somehow I feel these must endure;
Though I should not happen this way again,
These will persist, of these I am sure.

As an old man who, with increase of age,
Finds less and less necessity for sleep,
Knowing how soon it will be long and deep,
And so turns to the saint and to the sage
For truth to guide, for wisdom to assuage,
And on the sun and stars and winds that leap
And trees and birds and streams and stones that keep
So sweet a state, so pure an equipage
Leans more and more, as though these might bequeath
Their clarity and confidence, and so
Make him the worthier of love and death—
Even thus do I now greedily forego
The plumes of sleep, gathering all my breath
Against the glory of that double blow.

IMPONDERABLES

No less for me the morning's show
Lets the moon and planets glow;
Nor more His love than when there were
Saracens at the Sepulchre.

Equally musical is peace
When hornets loot the milky trees,
As when December's feathery doom
Furnishes a second bloom.

I find not pride nor passion less
For man's apparent helplessness;
Nor doubt his shadow on the moon
Will fade or flicker quite as soon.

Not vainly, nor for bread alone,
Does man in Nature's bounty forage:
He digs her beauty like a bone;
He buries it beneath a stone;
The little pine trees give him courage.

He thrusts his hand into the flame
Of truth; and hurls to headlong rout
Horrors the microscope must name;
And with a disk of glass will tame
The stars that blast his eyeballs out.

He plants his god upon a cliff;
He stands erect against some wall;
He sees the captain strained and stiff;
He waves away the handkerchief;
He settles to a gentle sprawl.

Beneath the banquet's doubtful worth
He taps a proud impatient shoe:
His heart is always bounding forth;
His eyes are always burning north.
We find the staring residue.

A blind and tawdry thing in death,
He dies before the rabble's shout,
Who, whilst he lived, poured lusty breath
That now could not disturb his wreath
Or puff one guttering taper out.

Or else he tunnels to the sun,
Or builds the tower he will take,
Whose paradox is never done,
Whom death's cold cheetah will outrun,
Whose breathlessness his heart will break.

The frozen tundra marks his grave;
A stick, a stone, a flag, or half
A line, or all of one vast wave,
A mattress, or a lion's cave
That roars his furious epitaph.

Yet, bedded snug or bedded ill,
Or bedless and a blowing dust,
He forages for beauty still,
His little pines ascend the hill,
He sleeps at length, and well, I trust.

Time, Dust, Darkness and the Spider
Make wine good and verses great:
Time the Decider and Dust the Hider
And Darkness full of dreams, and Fate
The velvet acrobat, the glider,
The Spider who knows how to wait.

I neither hope nor wish to shake
The world with any words of mine;
But I shall rest content to take
A single pebble for my sign,
And with a phrase as quiet break
The forehead of the Philistine.